Jesus Christ:
The Trinitarian God

THE ONLY SELF-MADE MAN

Nannette R. Heath

WESTBOW
P R E S S®
A DIVISION OF THOMAS NELSON
& ZONDERVAN

This material is taken from the Thompson Chain-Reference Bible with the permission of B.B. Kirkbride Bible Company.

Scripture taken from the King James Version of the Bible.

WestBow Press books may be ordered through booksellers or by contacting:

WestBow Press
A Division of Thomas Nelson & Zondervan
1663 Liberty Drive
Bloomington, IN 47403
www.westbowpress.com
1 (866) 928-1240

ISBN: 978-1-9736-4316-6 (sc)
ISBN: 978-1-9736-4317-3 (e)

Print information available on the last page.

WestBow Press rev. date: 01/18/2019

Locus: The place where something is situated or occurs: Site: The set of all points whose location is determined by stated conditions: The position on a chromosome of a particular gene or allele.
Allele: Any of the alternate forms of a gene that may occur at a given Locus: Location.
—*Merriam-Webster's Collegiate Dictionary*, Eleventh Edition
Locus: The place where God situates and occurs in eternity and in time.
Allele: Any of the forms of God, the Word. That may manifest at alternate or exact time(s). At a given locus: Location(s).
—Nannette R. Heath

Contents

Acknowledgments

First, I acknowledge Jesus Christ. He is my life. He is my Lord and my Savior. I also acknowledge Pete Nikolai, my group mentor hero of Elm Hill Press. He is also the director of publishing services at Harper Collins Christian Publishing. Thank you also to my lead publisher family *WestBow Press*. They are a division of Harper Collins Christian Publishing. I give respect to Quinita, who contributed specific editing services; to my dear sister Larita, who supports my theme; to my brother Kenneth, who was my protector and favorite playmate; to my eldest sister, Brenda, who was there for me during my childhood; and to all others who listened to my theory and gave knowledgeable feedback.

Author's Note and a Dialogue of Interactive Visions

Although this manuscript is not about those who have lost loved ones, I chose to dedicate a portion of this text to those who have. I therefore reverence my deceased, those ships that sailed by me. These ships add meaning to the song "I Stood on the Banks of Jordon." This song is so richly harmonized by Ranch Allen and the Temple of Deliverance Choir. These sentimental lyrics explain why I stood on the banks of Jordon. I stood there because "I had to see those ships go by." These ships include my father and mother, Willie and Nancy Heath; my siblings Lucius Heath and Myra A. Britton; and last, but not least, my great-niece Larissa Britton. My named loved ones continue to give more flavor and purpose to my life, even after death. This is God granting me the experience of an unexplained love plateau. This height of tangible passion is a gift of love, love that *only* God gives in times of such sickness and great loss. God knows. Maybe had I experienced this depth of love from my parents, I would have never wanted to leave their presences. With the granted love between my deceased and me, I dedicate this book to *all* who have lost loved ones. I offer you light and hope. I include three true interactive visions between my deceased. I also offer a fourth vision. This is an open-seeing vision supposedly experienced by Ray Charles. It may be true. Ray Charles's entry is first, and then the other three testimonies follow. These staged interactive visions with loved ones were no doubt staged of God. It is God who does for us the impossible, even after and in death.

With Encouragement from His Deceased, Ray Charles Was Delivered from Drugs!

Ray Charles was a blind African-American singer. He had an *open-seeing vision*. He was wide awake and walking around when his vision took place. And after his vision, he experienced a remarkable recovery from drugs. This encounter was true, according to his movie storyline. In his open-seeing vision, Ray was no longer a boy. He had become a man. He had had the experience of drugs. Ray's future recovery from drugs consisted of a verbal encounter with his deceased mother and brother. His mother implied to him that not even drugs could keep them apart. He placed his head in her lap. She soothed him gently. Suddenly, his brother came out of their childhood home. Ray Charles's brother had not aged. He was still a young boy. He was around five to seven years old. His brother approached him. Ray picked him up. His brother threw his arms around him. He said that his death by drowning in a large tin tub was not Ray's fault. Their verbal encouragements and warm embraces played a major role in Ray's deliverance from drugs. Sometime after that, Ray Charles left drugs alone. And his song "Georgia" was finally accepted as the theme song for the State of Georgia.

An Unusual Conversation, After Death!

I still can't believe my great-niece Larissa passed. I called her "Sugar Wooga." Her mother, Patrice Britton, had a vision. It was of herself and another daughter, Nykeya. They were sitting on a porch, talking to the deceased Larissa. Their mother said to Nykeya, "Nykeya, are we sitting on the porch talking to Larissa and Larissa is dead?"

Nykeya said something like, "Yeah …"

You Can Reap What You Sow in This World, Even in Death

We learn in the Bible "Be not deceived; God is not mocked: for whatsoever a man soweth, that shall he also reap" (Galatians 6:7 KJV). This happened to me in a vision. I was sleeping. I found myself having been lowered beyond normal. I was in an unfamiliar living room quarters. I found myself looking at a portal-type entrance. I said to myself, "When that door opens, Daddy is going to come in." While alive, Daddy would unexpectedly show himself at a few important events I participated in. After his death, God allowed me to visit him. Before his appearance, I hid. I hid behind the lounge chair. I hid because I had not seen him in so long. I did not know how I would respond upon seeing him, so I hid.

My mother had a real-life hiding experience. She had it with my living brother, Willie. Years before I entered active visions with Daddy, she informed me that she had hidden before his appearance. For the life of me, I could not understand why she had hidden from her own son. I asked her several times why she hid, even though she had insisted that she had hidden because she had not seen him in so long. She did not know how she would respond when he appeared, so she hid. My knowledge of Mother's real-life hiding encounter assured me that my hiding experience with Daddy had been real. The portal-type door did open, and in stepped Daddy.

Soon after his entrance, I sprang from behind the lounge chair. I said, "Hi, Daddy."

He said, "Hi, Nannette."

The lesson I learned was that you reap what you sow. It can happen to you in this lifetime and in death.

An Endless Love ...

Surely there is no love on the face of God's green earth like the love between a mother and her children. I loved my mother so much. I was anticipating the determination to expect to pray her back from the dead. I was to take time back to the eighties. Why the early eighties? This is when we had the opportunity to blossom as a family. At least that was how I perceived it when I contemplated changing the face of time. My mother was drop-dead gorgeous and sweet. She spoiled us, and it made our adult lives more complex than they should have been. Nevertheless, we adored her. When Mother would leave for work, my brother's love Jones for her poured down. He would get on the record player my father said he had purchased for me. He would spin the record for the song titled "I'll Always Love My Mother." Some of the words were "I will always love my mother. She's my favorite girl. I will always love my mother. She brought me in this world ..." This song was composed by the Intruders. Next, he would play "Sadie" by The Spinners.

My mother had had polio and would fall at times. One winter's day, Mother and Daddy went grocery shopping, as usual. The snows in Detroit in those days were unbearable. Mother told me that my brother, Willie, picked her up with the grocery bags. He carried both in the house and placed them down. I must mention Daddy's outward love for her. He was not her child but acted as such one day. Mother had gone to Winston Salem, North Carolina, for a visit. My sister Rita lived with our grandparents there. Mother had been gone a few days. Daddy sat in his chair, drunk. He acted as if Mother was never coming back. I attempted to soothe him. I said, "Daddy, Momma gone down south. She will be back."

He kept saying her name. He said, "Nancy, Nancy, where is Nancy?" He knew where she was. Then he looked over at me on the couch and said, "Go upstairs and get Nancy."

I was confused. I thought that was impossible. Well, after Mother had passed, I was determined to pray her back. I felt assured and confident. My mother soon came to me in a vision. I was in the kitchen on Lemay. She suddenly appeared in the living room. She proceeded to the outer door when I saw her. She stopped a few feet from my sister Rita, who stood in the doorway. I approached her. She said to me, "Nannette, you know that I am not here anymore. I have been through a lot. You know where I am." She soon faded out of sight. I no longer longed to pray her back.

Greetings From the Author, Nannette R. Heath

My name is Nannette. My reason for writing this book is to reveal that Jesus is God in His totality. He is God in His triune form. This revealing will also profess that He is also the only self-made man. The basis for this text is not doctrinal. It is written to shed great light on the preceding proclamations. The guiding light most prevalent to prove these facts is based on particular scriptures that confirm these truths. These scriptures certify that God, the Word, who is Jesus the Son, can be who He chooses and when.

There are several factors that give me authority to interpret the Word made flesh. These specifics include my spiritual history and its root, my spiritual insight, and the spiritual channels God has bestowed upon me. My spiritual journey also gives me this credibility. I am Apostolic in the concept that Jesus is the Trinitarian God. However, my spiritual root is the Church of God in Christ (COGIC). I am so very proud of my COGIC inheritance because it was there I found Jesus. I received His salvation. It was also there that God first wooed my heart. There, I was taught to be myself. I was commissioned to love the brethren. I was also instructed to allow God and His Word to have free course in my life. I became Apostolic because I unknowingly allowed the Spirit to guide me. This spiritual guidance revealed to me that Jesus is the Trinitarian God. He is the only self-made man. I still adhere to my COGIC roots, which I inherited of God. I also cling to God's Pentecostal direction for me. Therefore, I heed not doctrines but the teachings of the doctrines.

Introduction to the Thesis

It is expedient to peacefully say many limit God. For the most part, it is a doctrinal box people have sealed Him in. This is evident because many do not strive to get along with the whole body of Christ. I am referring to the saints who have the Spirit of Christ (Romans 8:9 KJV). These saints, the ones who have a different doctrine of God, are the ones set apart. This behavior interferes with understanding God in His totality. Many fail to study those scriptures that cross their doctrinal lines of Him. Many saints believe He is the Son. Therefore, He can't be God. And by the same token, He is God. How then can He be the Son? In their root in eternity, there is only God the Father and God the Word, who is the Son (John 1:1–2 KJV).

In this book, I shall confirm that God has no such conceived limitations. I shall rationalize how each Triune entity complements the others and together they interact as the Godhead bodily. I shall progress. I shall analyze the Word in His Triune attributes. I shall also note the biblical pictorial description of Jesus's Godhead body. My thesis statement shall showcase this path, the path I shall take to certify my title and stances on the locus. These concepts of the Word and the Godhead body shall be extracted from spiritual wells. One specific well I shall continually extract from is the Word of God, the Thompson Chain-Reference Bible, King James Version of the Bible (TCR-KJV) (1988), Fifth Improved Edition.

We also learn in the Thompson-Chain Reference Bible, "Behold a virgin shall be with child, and shall bring forth a son, and they shall call his name Emmanuel, which being interpreted is, *"God with us"* (Matthew 1:23 KJV, emphasis added). This scripture notarizes my story of Jesus's interpreted divinity. So stop, and take this dialogue back to my true godly experience. This testimony happened during devotional praise and worship. I stood near the center of my large, modern-day classroom. I applied a simple verbal example to the spiritual concept that Jesus is God. And this spiritual concept is "the revelation of Jesus Christ" (Revelation 1:1 KJV). This was my untold topic. This is evident because Jesus is the Trinitarian God seen in His fullness in Revelation 1:12–18. "For in him dwelleth all the fullness of the Godhead bodily" (Colossians 2:9 KJV). And that Godhead bodily consists of the Father, the Son, and the Holy Ghost. Therefore, Jesus Christ of Revelation is also He who is expressed in His fullness in Colossians 2:9. My mission was the interpreted unveiling and the revealing that Jesus is His spiritual root. He is "the set of all points." He is the locus, whose name is Logos, the self-created Word and "whose form and location is determined by stated conditions" (Merriam 2012). I am referring to God's genetic allele—specifically, any form and location of God the Word who "manifests at alternate or exact times" (Merriam 2012). These are His specific biblical and historical predestined forms. They are His locations and stated conditions of Him as the Word. And these concepts and traits of Jesus are His *history* and are connected to His preexisting need for Christ. I am radically articulating Christ's inheritance and preexisting calling. The Word's godly mission required particulars. His spiritual and physical traits were being an eternal, omnipresent, incarnate Jewish Rabbi Savior. For my students, I am bringing to life and light this theory that Jesus is indeed God. Without mention of the other named complexities of His Triune persona, my detailed account progressed similar to this.

"Class, what if you had an apple and another apple came from that same apple. How does this example entwine God and Jesus?" Suddenly, after multiple lapping seconds, one of the second-grade boys spoke. He chattered with great excitement. He loudly proclaimed that Jesus is God and the Son!

Thesis Statement and Continued Dialogue

But how can this mere mortal Jesus, biblically and interpretatively, declare both that He is the Trinitarian God and the only self-made man? And this progressive theology is the most controversial, contextual, and theoretical debate worthy of unfolding.

These statements of Jesus's divinity are true. They are equivalent to the revelation expressed of the student. The self-innate, undisputable truth that Jesus is God is given by the Spirit, or the direct will of God. My student's spiritual encounter is similar to Peter's stated revelations of Him. Peter's revelation was limited to the fact that Jesus is the Son of God. My student's revelation is similar in that both were given by the will of God. We learn in the Bible that God has "made known unto us the mystery of his will, according to his good pleasure which he hath purposed in himself" (Ephesians 1:9 KJV). For example, we learn in the Bible that

> When Jesus came into the coasts of Caesarea
> Philippi, he asked his disciples, saying, Whom
> do men say that I the Son of man am? And

they said, Some *say that thou art* John the Baptist: some, Elias; and others, Jeremias, or one of the prophets. He saith unto them, But whom say ye that I am? And Simon Peter answered and said, Thou art the Christ, the Son of the living God. And Jesus answered and said unto him, Blessed art thou, Simon Barjona: for flesh and blood hath not revealed it unto thee, but my Father which is in heaven. And I say also unto thee, That thou art Peter, and upon this rock I will build my church; and the gates of hell shall not prevail against it. (Matthew 16:13–18 KJV, emphasis added)

To my student, He revealed that the Father and the Son are one. Therefore, God reveals His mysteries to whom He will. He also reveals them to what extent He wills. God revealed to me that He is the Trinitarian God and the Only Self-Made Man.

Therefore, I shall continue my theological dialogue. I shall accomplish this with God's Spirit and Word. I shall prove one can grasp the concept that Jesus is the Trinitarian God and the Only Self-Made Man. References from God's Word shall defend my theoretical statements of Jesus's deity. I shall provide evidence for these interpreted theories from my personal spiritual experiences and sound Pentecostal teachings. I will also present song lyrics that reveal these interpreted truths.

This theoretical insight of Jesus is so magnificently exactly blueprinted in particular biblical scriptures. One of the most striking and profound scriptures of Jesus's divinity is John 8:42 (KJV). This scripture details and informs us of Jesus's self-implied eternal origin. Here, Jesus the Word declares, "I proceeded forth and came from God" (John 8:42 KJV). My spiritual interpretation perceived that I stepped out of God. Therefore, the Word certifies through Paul, John, and Matthew that Jesus is how God looks. We learn in the Bible that He "is the image of the invisible God" (Colossians 1:15 KJV, emphasis added). We also learn in the Bible that "In whom the god of this world hath blinded the minds of them which believe not, lest the light of the glorious gospel of Christ, *who is the image of God*, should shine unto them" (2 Corinthians 4:4, emphasis added). We also learn in the Bible that "*Who, being in the form of God*, thought it not robbery to be equal with God: But made himself of no reputation, and took upon him the form of a servant, and was made in the likeness of men" (Philippians 2:6–7 KJV, emphasis added). We also learn in the Bible that Jesus is "the brightness of his glory, and the expressed image of his person" (Hebrews 1:3). In addition, we also learn in the Bible that Jesus said, "And he that seeth me seeth him that sent me" (John 12:45 KJV) and that "This is the message which we have heard of him, and declare unto you, that God is light, and in him is no darkness at all" (1 John 1:5 KJV). God is pure. Therefore, Jesus can assert that I could not have treaded forth from God a generic prototype. And according to Colossians 1:16 (KJV), "For by him were all things created, that are in heaven, and that are in earth, visible and invisible, whether they be thrones, or dominions, or principalities, or powers: all things were created by him and for him" (says God the Word, emphasis added). We also learn in the Bible that "All things were made by him; and without him was not anything made that was made" (John 1:3 KJV). A relevant reference to (John 1:3) is 700 Christ, "The Word." This reference is located on the left side of (John 1:3) in the Thompson Chain Reverence Bible (TCR) (KJV). A second side reference to (John 1:3), in the same location is: (680) Christ, Creator). The biblically recorded fact that Jesus is creator of these specific entities defends Jesus's godship. A strong defense of the document that Jesus is God is recorded in the book of Isaiah. We learn in the Bible that "For unto us a child is born, unto us a son is given: and the government shall be upon his shoulder: and his name shall be called Wonderful, Counselor, *The mighty God, The ever lasting Father*, The Prince of Peace" (Isaiah 9:6 KJV, emphasis added). These scriptures strongly defend and state that Jesus is *the Word whose form is God*. They are also why I interpret particular transcending forms the Word manifests. For example, I interpret Jesus Christ of Revelation to be a self-made man. I also interpret that He wrapped Himself in flesh. He took on human flesh even then because Jesus Christ of Revelation is Spirit. His form then became similar to Melchisedec's, God being His own Priest. After all, who else can be God's Priest with no beginning and endless life (Hebrews 7:3)? I can also interpret then this transcended Ancient of Days pressed His needs in the dust. He gathered His dust to Himself. He formed His dirt man after His transcended self, the Trinitarian God. His dirt man's triune being is now compatible with their Godhead bodily. This dirt man's bodily forms consisted of body, spirit, and soul. "I beseech you therefore brethren, by the mercies of God, that ye present your bodies a living sacrifice, holy, acceptable unto God, *which* is your reasonable service" (Romans 12:1 KJV, emphasis added). We also learn in the Bible that "But *there is* a spirit in man …" (Job 32:8 KJV, emphasis added) and that "For what is a man profited, if he shall gain the whole world, and lose his own soul?" (Matthew 16:26, KJV).

> God said, Let us make man in our image, after our likeness: and let them have dominion over the fish of the sea, and over the fowl of the air, and over the cattle, and over all the earth, and over every creeping thing that creepeth upon the earth. So God created man in his *own image*, in the image of God created he him; male and female created he them. (Genesis 1:1–27 KJV, emphasis added)

Maybe while articulating to His Trinitarian Self, He also, in completion of His and man's domains, "blessed the seventh day, and sanctified it." We learn in the Bible that "God blessed the seventh day, and sanctified it: because that in it he had *rested* from all his work which *God created and made*" (Genesis 2:3 KJV, emphases added). The preceding sentences signify that Jesus and God are the same. First, this is evident because it was previously stated that Jesus created all things and that "without him was not anything made that was made." Second, it was implied that Jesus is God in stating that it was God who rested after all He had created and made.

These scriptures could be interpreted as the reason why Jesus recorded, "I and my Father are one" (John 10:30 KJV). I also interpret that before time existed, only these expressed two existed (John 1:2 KJV). Isaiah documents their existence before time or days. We read in the Bible, "Yea, *before the day was I am he* …" (Isaiah 43:13 KJV, emphasis added). A relevant reference to (Isaiah 43: 13) is 2481: God Eternal. This reference is located on the right side of (Isaiah 43:13) in the (TCR) (KJV). "Then said the Jews unto him, thou art not yet fifty years old, and hast thou seen Abraham? Jesus said unto them, Verily, verily, I say unto you, Before Abraham was, I am" (John 8:57–58 KJV). Did not God tell this to Moses? "And God said unto Moses, *I AM THAT I AM*: and he said, Thus shalt thou say unto the children of Israel, I AM hath sent me unto you" (Exodus 3:14 KJV, emphasis added).

> For when God made promise to Abraham, because *he could swear by no greater, he swear by himself,* Saying, Surely blessing I will bless thee, and multiplying I will multiply thee. And so, after he had patiently endured, he obtained the promise. (Hebrews 6:13 KJV, emphasis added).

His self consists of His twine one, God and God the Word. David speaks of their omnipresence. David said, "If I ascend up into heaven, thou *art* there: if I make my bed in hell, behold, thou *art there. If* I take the wings of the morning, and dwell in the uttermost parts of the sea; Even there shall thy hand lead me, and thy right hand shall hold me" (Psalm 139:8–10, emphasis added). A side reference to (Psalm 139: 8 - 10) is (2645): Omnipresence. This reference is located on the right side of (Psalm 139: 8-10) in the (TCR) (KJV). Therefore, God the Father and God the Word have all power and are omnipresent. We have biblically established that the Word and God have an everlasting domain and that they are also omnipresent. These two conclusions are based on the previous biblical facts. In these conclusions, it is also interpreted that they occupy an unstated eternal domain. We have biblically acknowledged that God and God the Word existed before time. But not the root where their eternal dwelling is. And so, it is this Word who is in the bosom of God and is also in the root of eternity with God. Therefore, the Word and God are one. This is before the heavens. This is before the angels. This is before principalities. This is also before the forming of the stars. They dwell somewhere and someplace in the Spirit's and the Word's domain. Perhaps it is in the mind of God. This is where the Word did transcend self. This is the ability to metamorphose one's own deity. "And the Word illuminated forward, out of the bosom of God, in the deity of the Ancient of Days" (Daniel 7:9 KJV). He is the only begotten Son of God, a Spirit-man.

Jesus said, "And unto the angel of the church in Thyatira write; These things saith the Son of God, who hath his eyes like unto a flame of fire, and his feet are like fine brass" (Revelation 2:18 KJV). The scripture in Revelation 2:18 KJV confirms that Jesus was the Son of God in heaven before Mary conceived Him of His Holy Ghost. Paul also confirms this theory that Jesus was Son in heaven before

He was the Son on earth. "For what the law could not do, in that it was weak through the flesh, *God sending his own Son in the likeness of sinful flesh*" (Romans 8:3 KJV, emphasis added). We read in the Bible, "I will declare the decree: the Lord hath said unto me, Thou *art* my Son; this *day* have I begotten thee" (Psalm 2:7 KJV, emphasis added). Interpreting, God named him the Ancient of Days. And according to another of David's interpreted prophecies, David implied Jesus said to the Father that "*A body hast thou prepared me*" (Hebrews 10:5 KJV, emphasis added). I am not saying that David was not also prophesying about or to the man Christ Jesus but that David was first referring to the Ancient of Days. So, let us resolve the fact that the Man Christ Jesus had not yet been born when David's proclamations were made. The Ancient of Days had long manifested. We learn in the Bible that "[i]n him was life and the life was the light of men" (John 1:4 KJV). The life and light that were in the Ancient of Days was Himself, Jesus Christ the Man. We also learn in the Bible that "He was in the world, and *the world was made by him* and the world knew him not" (John 1:10 KJV, emphasis added).

> And *the Word was made flesh*, and dwelt among us, (and we beheld his glory, the glory as of the only begotten of the Father) full of grace and truth … but as many as received him, to them gave he power to become the sons of God, *even* to them that believe on *his name*: Which were born, not of blood, nor of

the will of the flesh, nor of the will of man, but of God. (John 1:11–13 KJV, emphasis added)

Thus, these biblical interpretations mean that the Ancient of Days was in the world, a man. This Word became flesh to define His preordained Hebrew genealogy. "For *there is* one God, and one mediator between God and men, the man Christ Jesus" (1 Timothy 2:5 KJV, emphasis added). As stated, this is the same Jesus whose eyes are as a flame of fire in Revelation 19:12, although His earthly appearance had transcended to that of Jewish descent (Matthew 1:1 KJV). And Jesus's physical form in Daniel and His name (changed in Revelation 1:1 KJV) can visibly be matched to and clearly seen in the person of Jesus Christ of Revelation. And the preceding scriptures of Jesus in Daniel 7:9 KJV and Revelation 1:13–15 authenticate that the Ancient of Days was already the Son before His earthly conception. And this begotten Son's statements of His earthly birth positioned Him to be the only self-made man and Savior of the world. This prophetic ratiocinating fellowship between the twine is unique. For God the Word became the Son. He has no ascendants or descendants of His eternal root. And all other beings and kinds after the Son were either created or made by Him, God the Word (Colossians 1:16). Therefore, He created and made those creations and manifestations that are clarified in Genesis 1:1–31 KJV)—even Satan, as is expressed in Ezekiel 28:13–16. We learn that God said this to Satan:

Thou hast been in Eden the garden of God; every precious stone *was* thou covering, the sardius, topaz, and the diamond, the beryl, the onyx; and the jasper, the sapphire, the emerald, and the carbuncle, and gold: the workmanship of thy tabrets and of thy pipes was prepared in thee in the day that thou was created. Thou *art* the anointed cherub that covereth; and I have set thee so: thou wast upon the holy mountain of God; thou hast walked up and down in the midst of the stone of fire. Thou *wast* perfect in thy ways from the day that thou wast created, till iniquity was found in thee. By the multitude of thy merchandise they have filled the midst of thee with violence, and thou has sinned: therefore I will cast thee as profane out of the mountain of God: and I will destroy thee, O covering cherub, from the midst of the stones of fire. (Ezekiel 28:13–16 KJV, emphasis added)

Leaving Satan's fate, let's redirect our focus to the fellowship of the Father and the Son. God the Father and Jesus the Son's twine ship are so distinctly incomparable to an earthly father and son's kinship. After Adam and Eve, a father and son have earthly ascendants and descendants. They have genetics from the two bloodlines of their father and their mother. They also often have strong physical characteristics of unseen ascendants. This is unlike the twine ship of the Father and the Son, whose genetic root is one.

> Thou, *even* thou, *art* Lord alone; thou hast made heaven, the heaven of heavens, with all their host, the earth, and all *things* that *are* therein, the seas, and all that *is* therein, and thou preservest them all; and the host of heaven worshippeth thee. Thou *art* the Lord the God, who didst choose Abram, and broughtest him forth out of Ur of the Chaldees, and gavest him the name of Abraham. (Nehemiah 9:6–7 KJV, emphasis added)

Remember Jesus said in Colossians 1:16 that He created all things in heaven. It is also stated in John 1:3. He is the sole maker of all made things. We also learn in the Bible that Jesus said, "Ye are from beneath; I am from above, ye are of this world; I am not of this world" (John 8:23 KJV). These are some biblical and historical informative facts about Him. They also entail some forms, locations, and redemptive stated conditions about Him. They connote what the Spirit says about its history and man. And the preceding scriptures proclaim God's self. They signify God's absolute powers and supreme authority, God's sovereignty and who and where He chooses to be. They also detail when God chooses to be at specific places through the application of Himself the Word. And these events are also why one would comprehend that Jesus is the locus called Logos. Logos is accepted as the second person *separating* His Godhead bodily. *Merriam-Webster's Collegiate Dictionary* defines the words *locus* and *logos*. The definition for locus has been given. The definition for *logos* is "The divine wisdom manifest in the creation, government, and redemption of the world." Logos is "often identified with the second person of the Trinity" and (historically) is the "reason that in ancient Greek philosophy is the controlling principle in the universe" (Merriam 2012). Trinitarians worldwide perceive Jesus's positional status as such. The Church of God in Christ defends His Trinity in their "Statement of Faith." They affirm that "We believe that Jesus is the son of God." He "is the second person in the Godhead of the trinity or Triune Godhead" (www.gstcogic.org). Bible. org's theology of Jesus is aligned similarly to COGIC's "Statement of Faith." Under their website titled *The Nature of God*, they state, "There is one God who in His unity, expresses Himself tri personally as Father, Son, and Holy Spirit. Each member of the Godhead is coequal and one in sub-stance, but separate in subsistence" ("Theology: The Doctrine of God"). This trinity, the dividing of the three, is biblically documented in the commission of the Godhead body. In the Word of God, the Father (who is a Spirit) is manifest in His commission to fulfill His office as the Father. The Son, who is also the Man Christ Jesus, is manifest in His commission to fulfill His office as the Son. The Holy Ghost, who is the power of God, is also manifest in His commission to fulfill His office as the power of God, who gets the job done. For example, the following are some of their commissions:

1. Biblical Commissions of the Spirit of God (the Father)

- Jesus read in the book of Isaiah that "The Spirit of the Lord is upon me; because the Lord hath anointed me to preach good tidings unto the meek; he hath sent me to bind up the broken-hearted, to proclaim liberty to the captives, and the opening of the prison to *them that are bound*" (Isaiah 61:1 KJV, emphasis added).

- "God *is* a Spirit: and they that worship him must worship *him* in spirit and in truth" (John 4:24 KJV, emphasis added).

- "For as many as are led by the Spirit of God, they are the sons of God" (Romans 8:14 KJV).

- "But for the fruit of the Spirit is love, joy, peace, longsuffering, gentleness, goodness, faith, Meekness, temperance: against such there is no law. And they that are Christ's have crucified the flesh with the affections and lusts" (Galatians 5:22–24 KJV).

- "That the God of our Lord Jesus Christ, the Father of glory, may give unto you the spirit of wisdom and revelation in the knowledge of him" (Ephesians 1:17 KJV).

- "That he would grant you, according to the riches of his glory, to be strengthened with might by his Spirit in the inner man; That Christ may dwell in your hearts by faith; that ye, being rooted and grounded in love, May be able to comprehend with all saints what is the breadth, and length, and depth, and height; And to know the love of Christ, which passeth knowledge, that ye might be filled with all the fulness of God" (Ephesians 3:16–19 KJV).

- "For God hath not given us the spirit of fear; but of power, and of love, and of a sound mind" (2 Timothy 1:7 KJV).

2. Biblical Commissions of Jesus Christ (The Son)

- "Now when Jesus was born in Bethlehem of Judaea in the days of Herod the king, behold, there came wise men from the east to Jerusalem, Saying, Where is he that is born King of the Jews? For we have seen his star in the east, and are come to worship him" (Matthew 2:1–2 KJV).

- "Then was Jesus led up on the Spirit into the wilderness to be tempted of the devil" (Matthew 4:1 KJV).

- "But he answered and said, It is written, Man shall not live by bread alone, but by every word that proceedeth out of the mouth of God" (Matthew 4:4 KJV).

- "And Jesus went about all Galilee, teaching in the synagogues, and preaching the gospel of the kingdom, and healing all manner of sickness and all manner of disease among the people" (Matthew 4:23 KJV).

- "Judge not, that ye be not judged" (Matthew 7:1 KJV).

- "Then said Jesus unto his disciples, If any *man* will come after me, let him deny himself, and take up his cross, and follow me" (Matthew 16:24, emphasis added).

- "The Son of man must suffer many things, and be rejected of the elders and chief priests and scribes, and be slain, and be raised the third day" (Luke 9:22 KJV).

3. Commissions of the Holy Ghost (The Power of God)

- "(Mary) was found with child of the Holy Ghost," and the child was Jesus (Matthew 1:18 KJV).

- "If ye love me, keep my commandments. And I will pray the Father, and he shall give you another Comforter, that he may abide with you for ever" (John 14:16 KJV).

- We learn in the Bible who the Comforter is: "But the Comforter, which is the Holy Ghost, whom the Father will send in my name, he shall teach you all things, and bring all things to your remembrance, whatsoever I have said unto you" (John 14:26 KJV).

- Jesus stated, "But when the Comforter is come, whom I will send unto you from the Father, even the Spirit of truth, which proceeded from the Father, he shall testify of me" (John 15:26 KJV).

- "Nevertheless I tell you the truth: It is expedient for you that I go away: for if I go not away, the Comforter will not come unto you; but if I depart, *I will send him unto you*" (John 16:7 KJV, emphasis added).

- "For the kingdom of God is not meat and drink; but righteousness, peace, and joy in the Holy Ghost" (Romans 14:17 KJV).

- "[T]he Holy Ghost descended in a bodily shape like a dove upon him, and a voice came from heaven, which said, Thou art my beloved Son; in thee I am well pleased" (Luke 3:22 KJV).

- "[T]he Holy Ghost shall teach you in the same hour what you ought to say" (Luke 12:12 KJV).

- Paul asked Ephesus's disciples, "Have ye received the Holy Ghost since ye believed?" (Acts 19:2 KJV).

- "Wherefore (as the Holy Ghost saith, To day if ye will hear his voice, Harden not your hearts" (Hebrews 3:7 KJV).

Jesus, the Locus

Although each "body" in the Trinity operates on a separate commission, they remain one living being, Jesus. This is according to Colossians 2:9. "[Y]e are complete in him, which is the head of all principality and power" (Colossians 2:9–10 KJV). I will further interpret this of the twine one. God is Spirit. Therefore God's Son has to be God's Spirit. These biblical facts about Jesus are also confirmations that Jesus was divine and human. However, in His resurrection, He was raised in Spirit form. Stay with me; I am going somewhere explaining the genetics of Jesus. "There is a natural body, and there is a spiritual body. It is sown a natural body; it *is raised a spiritual body*" (1 Corinthians 15:44 KJV, emphasis added). We also learn in the Bible that "flesh and blood cannot inherit the kingdom of heaven" (1 Corinthians 15:50 KJV).

> For this corruptible must put on incorruption, and this mortal *must* put on immortality. So when this corruptible shall have put on incorruption, and this mortal *must* put on immortality, then shall be brought to pass the saying that is written, death is swallowed

up in victory. (1 Corinthians 15:53–54 KJV, emphasis added).

Jesus has no sin. He did not have to take off corruption, as it was he "Who did no sin, neither was guile found in his mouth: Who, when he was reviled, reviled not again; when he suffered, he threatened not; but committed *himself* to him that judgeth righteously" (1 Peter 2:22–23 KJV, emphasis added). Jesus's divinity is God, and this made Him immortal. Therefore, Jesus did not have to put on immortality. He just had to rise in His immutability, which is God raising Him. I interpret that as God *in* Jesus the man. He raised Jesus from the dead. "But what saith it? The word is nigh thee, even in thy mouth, and in thy heart: that is, the word of faith, which we preach." That if thou shalt confess with thy mouth the Lord Jesus, and shalt believe in thine heart that God hath raised him from the dead, thou shalt be saved" (Romans 10:8–10 KJV). If you continue in His Word, you shall be His.

Therefore, it is biblically possible that God's Spirit that is Jesus raised Jesus the man from the dead. Let's review John 10:17–18. Jesus says,

> Therefore doth my Father love me, because I lay down my life, that I might take it again. No man taketh it from me, but I lay it down of myself. I have power to lay it down, and *I have power to take it again.* This commandment have I received of my Father. (John 10:17–18 KJV, emphasis added)

And so, God's Spirit, preasserted, is this mortal man raised in Spirit form. These are some causes in which Jesus's prophetic will is to reign over a people. It is to rule over a geotropic kingdom called new heaven and earth. Jesus's will to reign over these entities is also found in Daniel, which states,

> I saw in the night visions, and, behold, one like the Son of man came with the clouds of heaven, and came to the Ancient of days, and they brought him near before him. And there was given him dominion, and glory, and a kingdom, that all people, nations, and languages, should serve him: his dominion is an everlasting dominion, which shall not pass away, and his kingdom that which shall not be destroyed. (Daniel 7:13–14 KJV)

We also read in the Bible:

> And I saw a new heaven and a new earth: for the first heaven and the first earth were passed away; and there was no more sea. And I John saw the holy city, new Jerusalem, coming down from God out of heaven, prepared as a bride adorned for her husband. And I heard a great voice out of heaven saying, Behold, the tabernacle of God *is* with men, and he will dwell with them, and they shall be his people, and God himself shall be with them, *and be* their God. And God shall wipe away all tears

from their eyes; and there shall be no more death, neither sorrow, nor crying neither shall there be any more pain: for the former things are passed away. And he that sat upon the throne said, Behold, I make all things new. (Revelation 21:1–5 KJV, emphasis added)

These biblical facts are inclusive for the Apocalypse for Himself and humankind. Salvation then becomes about the redemption of a dirt man, Adam and the now bone of (his) bones and flesh of (his) flesh. This is Adam's wife, Eve (Genesis 2:23 KJV, emphasis added). Ladies, God created for Adam a gorgeous, shapely woman. God is a God of beauty and splendor. I believe this without thought or doubt. "And Adam called his wife's name Eve; because she was the mother of all living" (Genesis 3:20 KJV). At this time, being secluded in the Garden of Eden, yes, they became corrupt. They needed a Savior, after a decisive fall. God and the Word knew in their eternity that man would never be able to self-redeem. So, the Word emanated forth (John 1:18 KJV). He manifested in His royal tailored garb: His Trinitarian anatomy, the Godhead body (Revelation 1:13–16). And He brought time and days into existence. He also received the name relevant to time and days, the Ancient of Days. No doubt, He is a Spirit. He is God. He has distinctive spiritual physical features and transcending powers. These specific stated visible and invisible pictorial details are the locus, especially those of Him in Ezekiel 1:26, Daniel 7:9, and Revelation 1:12–18. The pictorial details in these books are Him. The stated images of His Spiritual-physical forms throughout Revelation are Him. These are expressed images of Jesus Christ, the Trinitarian God. All such stated scripture are Him. It is He, whether His form and location is appearing sitting on His throne alone. This is true. John recorded, "And immediately I was in the spirit: and, behold, a throne was set in heaven, and *one* sat on the throne. And he that sat was to look like a jasper and a sardine stone" (Revelation 4:2–3 KJV, emphasis added). It is also He who spoke to the light. God said, "Let there be light: and there was light" (Genesis 1:3 KJV). And it is also He who sought to have fellowship with Adam and Eve in the cool of the day. "And they heard the *voice of the Lord God walking* in the garden in the cool of the day: and Adam and his wife hid themselves *from the presences of the Lord God* amongst the trees of the garden" (Genesis 3:8 KJV, emphasis added). And it is also the same He who appeared to Abraham in the plains of Mamre while he sat in his tent door, in the heat of the day. "God appeared unto him in the plains of Mamre: and he sat in the tent door in the heat of the day" (Genesis 18:1 KJV). We also learn in the Bible that "Unto thee it was shewed, that thou mightiest know that the Lord he *is* God; *there is* none else beside him" (Deuteronomy 4:35 KJV, emphasis added). It is yet He who is God of gods. "For the Lord your God *is* God of gods, and Lord of lords, a great God, a mighty, and a terrible, which regardeth not persons, nor taketh reward" (Deuteronomy 10:17 KJV, emphasis added). This is the same He who requires us to obey His voice.

And it shall come to pass, if ye shall hearken diligently unto my commandments which I command you this day, to love the Lord your God, and to serve him with all your heart and with all your soul. That I will give *you* the rain of your land in his due season, the first rain and the latter rain, that thou mayest gather in thy corn, and thy wine, and thine oil. And I will send grass in thy fields for thy cattle, that thou mayest eat and be full. (Deuteronomy 11:13–15 KJV, emphasis added)

It is also He who articulated his divinity to Martha. "Jesus said unto her, I am the resurrection and the life" (John 11:25 KJV). And no doubt, in Revelation 1:12–16 KJV, it is He wearing His Trinitarian diadem. John said,

And I turned to see the voice that spake with me. And being turned, I saw seven golden candle sticks; and in the midst of the seven candle sticks *one* like unto the Son of man, clothed with a garment down to the foot, and girt about the paps with a golden girdle. His head and *his* hairs were white like wool, as white as snow; and his eyes *were* as a flame of fire; And his feet like unto fine brass, as if they burned in a furnace; and his voice as the sound of many waters. And he had in his right hand seven stars: and out of his mouth went a sharp twoedged sword: and his countenance *was* as the sun shineth in his strength. (Revelation 1:12–16 KJV, emphasis added)

This is Melchisedec, who abides forever. We learn in the Bible that Melchisedec is "[w]ithout father, without mother, without descent, having neither beginning of days, nor end of life; but made like unto the Son of God; abideth a priest continually" (Hebrews 7:3 KJV). And Melchisedec is he who met Levi while he was still in the loins of his father, Jacob. "For he was yet in the loins of his father, when Melchisedec met him" (Hebrews 7:10 KJV). He is the transcending Word, although His name is Melchisedec. And also, it is He when He is the slain Lamb of God. John recorded, "And I beheld, and lo, in the midst of the throne and of the four beasts, and in the midst of the elders, stood a Lamb as it had been slain, having seven horns and seven eyes, (which the seven Spirits of God are) sent forth into all the earth" (Revelation 5:6 KJV). The transcending Word is also He, "the same Lamb" who was capable of loosing the seven seals. We learn in the Bible that the Lamb was he who "came and took the book out of the right hand of him that sat upon the throne" (Revelation 5:7 KJV). "And when he had taken the book, the four and twenty elders fell down before the Lamb, having every one of them harps, and golden vials full of odours, which are the prayers of saints" (Revelation 5:8 KJV). John recorded many, many centuries later that "The next day John seeth Jesus coming unto him, and saith, Behold the Lamb of God, which taketh away the sin of the world" (John 1:29 KJV). Integrating further, it is also He who bowed the heavens while coming to earth. "He *bowed the heavens also*, and came down: and darkness was under his feet" (Psalm 18:9 KJV, emphasis added). He is the Lord who is scheduled to return to earth, to fight and to redeem.

> And *his feet shall stand in that day upon the mount of olives*, which is before Jerusalem on the east, and the mount of Olives shall cleave in the midst there of toward the east and toward the west, and there shall be a very great valley; and half of the mountain shall remove toward the north, and half of it toward the south. (Zechariah 14:4 KJV, emphasis added)

> And ye shall flee to the valley of the mountains; for the valley of the mountains shall reach unto Azal: yea, ye shall flee, like as ye fled from before the earthquake in the days of Uzziah king of Judah: *and the Lord my God shall come, and all the saints with thee.* (Zechriah 14:5 KJV, emphasis added)

> And it shall come to pass, *that* every one that is left of all the nations which came against Jerusalem shall even go up from year to year to worship the King, the Lord of hosts, and to keep the feast of tabernacles. And it shall be, *that* whoso will not come up of *all* the families of the earth unto Jerusalem to worship the King, the Lord of hosts, even upon them shall

be no rain. And if the family of Egypt go not up, and come not, that *have* no *rain*; there shall be the plague, wherewith the Lord will smite the heathen that come not up to keep the feast of tabernacles. This shall be the punishment of Egypt, and the punishment of all nations that come not up to keep the feast of tabernacles. (Zechariah 14:16–19 KJV)

Jehovah alone is his name (Psalm 83:18 KJV). And it is this same Word who sits on the white throne. John also said, "And I saw a great white throne, and him that sat on it, from whose face the earth and the heaven fled away" (Revelation 20:11 KJV). Jesus aggressively asserted that he is God in Revelation 1:18. Jesus affirmed, "I *am he that liveth, and was dead*; and, behold, I am alive for evermore, Amen; and have the keys of hell and of death" (Revelation 1:18 KJV, emphasis added). It is also He who states that upon his servants, after the conclusion of this world, will be written his "new name." We learn in the Bible that "Him that over cometh will I make a pillar in the temple of my God, and he shall go no more out: and I will write upon him the name of my God, and the name of the city of my God, which is new Jerusalem … and I will write upon him my new name" (Revelation 3:12 KJV). All are God, the transcending Word who remains unseen in the bosom of God (John 1:18). From an even deeper self-perspective of these interpreted truths, what if you were God a Spirit and God the Word? Let us say that you are God, a Spirit, and God the Word. Let us say that you have such infinite, self-forming, transcending spiritual powers. Tell me, would you eternally aspire and be a man?

These allegations, interpreting some forms and locations of the Word, are some reasons why He is this locus. He is the one about whom the boy was enlightened during the second-grade worship lecture. He is as interpreted, God, the prophetic. This is why it is understood that in the mind of God, all things have already come to pass. All spiritual concepts have already transpired before their existence. This also includes the preparation of God as a man.

A viewpoint that I have expressed about the deity of Jesus is also shared by Richard F. Ames. Mr. Ames is the editorial director of *Tomorrow's World*, a magazine that keeps us abreast of End Time prophesies. In one of their editorial editions, Richard A. Ames documented a quote from Zechariah 14:8–9. He prophetically confirms,

> We are now in the prophesied period known as the end-time. We need to prepare for the Second Coming. Christ will be King over all the earth, ruling from the new world capital, Jerusalem. And in that day it shall be that living waters shall flow from Jerusalem; half of them toward the eastern sea and half of them toward the western sea; in both summer and winter it shall occur. And the Lord shall be King over all the earth. In that day it shall be—"The Lord is one, and His name one." (Tomorrow's World, 2014).

There are interpreted prophetic revelations that I have about the Logos and these "living waters." They entail the worshipping of the Lord during His millennium reign. All *converts* who worship the King during His millennium reign shall receive the Holy Ghost. These converts shall receive the Holy Ghost after having drunk of water because these "living waters" shall have engulfed all water. I believe that these living waters shall also have healing powers. This is relevant to (John 5:2) and (John 7:38). A reference to these two scriptures is (3789) which is located in the "CONDENSED CYCLOPEDIA of TOPICS and TEXTS" section in the (TCR) (KJV). The Apostolic song "The Water Way" is a confirmation of the saving properties of these "living waters." I interpret this from a song by Sister Hattie Edwards. The song is "The Water Way." One can imply that Sister Hattie Edwards' song certifies that converts shall receive the Holy Ghost after having drunk of these "living waters." Her song confirms that if young and old repent of sins, the Holy Ghost shall come in. The Holy Ghost shall manifest in converts through "The Water Way." This song is taken from Zechariah 14:8–9. This is when Christ shall return "in the evening time," as she and Zechariah assert. And this is also when all shall know that God and Christ are one. The fact that God and Christ are one is evident because we learn in the Bible that "in the day of the Lord, in that day shall there be one Lord and his name one" (Zechariah 14:9). Therefore, all such Baptisms and healings shall be given and received in His name (Zechariah 14:9). During Christ's millennium reign, the Lord Himself shall be our Spirit guide. And, no doubt, Christ will be revealed as the present, returning living Word. These precepts I have dissected of the Word of God are based on my interpretation of the written Word of God.

The following are additional proof of Christ's divinity, and they are reflective of his Trinitarian reign. These concepts of Jesus are initially based on biblical documentations and side references of the Thompson Chain-Reference Bible, King James Version of the Bible. They include but are not limited to Isaiah 6:1, Daniel 7:13, Revelation 1:17, and Revelation 20:11. And these are evident in the Word's transcending powers. The selected scriptures are as follows.

Side References of the Divinity of Christ and Continued Dialogue

Isaiah 6:1

1. 3418—God's throne (TCR)
2. 1164—God exalted (TCR)

Daniel 7:13–14, Transcending

1. 722—Son of Man (TCR)
2. 1344—Second Coming (TCR)
3. 2483—Eternal Kingdom (TCR)
4. 718—Christ Exalted (TCR)
5. 683—Christ's Glory (TCR)
6. 3421—Christ King (TCR)
7. 717—Christ's Dominion (TCR)
8. 2483—Eternal Kingdom (TCR)
9. 2480—Immutability (TCR)

Visions of the Glorified Christ

1. 709—Christ Eternal (TCR)

Revelation 20:11—The Ancient of Days (Jesus Christ), the Trinitarian God

> And I saw a great white throne, *and him that sat on it*, from *whose face* the earth and heaven fled away; and there was found no place for them. And I saw the dead small and great, *stand before God*; and the books were open; and another book was open, which is *the book* of life: and the dead were judged out of those things which were written in the books, according to their works. (KJV, emphasis added)

Reference of Revelation 20:11—Continue with the Last Judgment of Him That Sitteth on the Throne: The Ancient of Days

1. 3418—God's Throne (TCR)
2. 2234—God's Majesty (TCR)
3. 2479—Mutability (p.p. Da.2:35) (TCR)
4. 1354—God, a Judge (p.p. Da. 7:10) (TCR)

These reverence visions of the Glorified Christ and are noted as Christ eternal (709) (TCR). This reference statement also confirms that Jesus is the eternal Word.

To prove that He is "the glorified Christ" and to showcase his root from this peripheral view, I have listed seven referenced scriptures. These scriptures are taken from John 1:1–4, and the referenced confirmations of John 1:1–4 are located on this scripture's left side, the TCR section of the KJV. They are as follows:

1. 700—Christ "the Word" (TCR)
2. 709—Christ Eternal (TCR)
3. 702—Christ Divine (TCR)
4. 709—Preexistence of Christ (TCR)
5. 680—Christ Creator (TCR)
6. 2152—Christ the Life (TCR)
7. 2168—Christ the Light (TCR)

These references contain scriptures that identify Christ God.

Jesus Christ Is God!

And to give more solid biblical and historical support that Jesus, this Christ, is God, consider what Paul has recorded. "And without controversy great is the mystery of godliness: God was manifest in the flesh, justified in the Spirit, seen of angels, preached unto the Gentiles, believed on in the world, received up into glory" (1 Timothy 3:16 KJV). A specific reference to 1 Timothy 3:16 (KJV) is located on the right side of the TCR-KJV) of the Bible, and it states the "ascension of Christ" (678). This reference statement interprets this scripture to mean that Christ is God who "was manifest in the flesh." Christ is God who was "justified in the Spirit." Christ is God who "was seen of angels" and "preached unto the Gentiles." Christ is God who was "believed on in the world" and "received up into glory." Jesus Himself further affirms that He is God in Revelation

1:8 (KJV). We learn in the Bible that Jesus confirms, "I am Alpha and … Omega, saith the Lord, *which is, and which was, and which is to come* the Almighty" (Revelation 1:8 KJV, emphasis added). One reference to this scripture is God Eternal/2481:11:17 (TCR). This reference is located on the scripture's left side in the TCR-KJV. These references authenticate that Jesus is God. John of Revelation records the hosts of God giving the same accolades to God as Jesus proclaimed of Himself in Revelation 1:8. This proclamation of Jesus and God occurs in Revelation 11:16–17. "And the four and twenty elders, which sat before God on their seats, fell upon their faces, and worshiped God, Saying, We give thee thanks, O Lord God Almighty, *which art, and wast, and art to come;* because thou hast taken to thee thy great power, and hast reigned" (Revelation 11:16–17 KJV, emphasis added). And an identical right side reference to both scriptures includes God Eternal (2481) (TCR). Another reference number to this scripture is 3419 (TCR), which is God King. This statement identifies God and Jesus as one.

The Coexistence of the Twine One: The Father and the Son

Now it is expedient to discuss, in more depth, the oneness of the Father and the Son. Isaiah boldly defends the oneness of the Father and the Son. Isaiah asserted that "God calls to Cyrus for his church's sake." God instructs them to

Assemble yourselves and come; draw near together, ye *that are* escaped of the nations:

they have no knowledge that set up the wood of their graven images, and pray unto a god *that* cannot save. Tell ye, and bring *them* near; yea, let them take counsel together: who hath declared this from ancient time? *who* hath told it from that time? *have* not I the Lord? and *there is no God else beside me; a just God and a Saviour*; *there is* none beside me. (Isaiah 45:20–21 KJV, emphasis added)

It is clear that God and Jesus are frequently discussed interchangeably as the same deity in the scripture. And another compelling and profound scripture that greatly defends this is in the book of Revelation. John recorded,

And I saw as it were a sea of glass mingled with fire: and them that had gotten the victory over the beast, and over his image, and over his mark, *and* over the number of his name, stand on the sea of glass, having the harps of God. And they sing the song of Moses the servant of God, and the song of the Lamb, saying, Great and marvelous *are* thy works, *Lord God Almighty, just and true are thy ways, thou King of saints*. (Revelation 15:2–3 KJV, emphasis added)

Now, it is expedient to discuss another interesting passage that gives rise to the complexity of the Father and the Son, and this is found in the book of Isaiah. This is the passage in which the word *Lord* is used to imply that Jesus and God are one and the same. Isaiah confirms this in the book of Isaiah. Isaiah recorded,

> Ye *are* my witnesses, saith the Lord, and my servant whom I have chosen; that ye may know and believe me, and understand that I *am* he: *before me there was no God formed, neither shall there be after me.* I, even I, *am* the Lord; and *beside me there is no savior.* I have declared, and have saved, and I have shewed, when *there was* no strange *god* among you: therefore ye *are* my witnesses, saith the Lord, that I *am God.* (Isaiah 43:10–12 KJV, emphasis added)

Traits of the Trinity

Now, I shall discuss traits of the Trinity. This concept involves acknowledging through biblical examples that Jesus Christ of Revelation, the Ancient of Days, and the Son of Man are the same Being. I shall do this to excel to more advanced biblically interpreted facts as to why Jesus is His eternal root. The three specific scriptures that identify this fact are located in Daniel 7:9, Revelation 1:14, and Matthew 8:20. Daniel recorded, "I beheld till the thrones were cast down, and the Ancient of days did sit, whose garment *was* white as snow, *and the hair on his head like the pure wool*" (Daniel 7:9 KJV, emphasis added). John recorded similar descriptions of Jesus Christ's head of hair in the book of

Revelation. "His head and his hairs were white like wool, as white as snow" (Revelation 1:14 KJV, emphasis added). A Famous End Time spokesperson also asserts that Jesus Christ is the Ancient of Days. During his TV telecast, he bluntly blurted out, "Jesus Christ, the Ancient of Days" (TV 2017).

To press forward with this concept of Jesus, I must biblically reveal that Jesus Christ is also the Man Christ Jesus. "And Jesus saith unto him, The foxes have holes, and the birds of the air *have* nests; but *the Son of man* hath not where to lay *his* head" (Matthew 8:20 KJV, emphasis added). We have just confirmed that Jesus Christ is the Ancient of Days and the Son of Man. The Word of God has not only power to coexist; it also has power to occupy the same space at the same time. Daniel certifies this; he details *the Son of man* coming to the Ancient of Days. "I saw in the night vision, and, behold, *one* like the Son of man came with the clouds of heaven, and came to the Ancient of days, and they brought him near before him" (Daniel 7:13 KJV, emphasis added). These biblical examples inform us that the transcendent Word is coexisting and occupying the same space and at the same time. Ezekiel also depicts this truth: the power of the Word to coexist and to occupy the same space. This coexistence and the occupying of the same space by the Word is also expressed in Ezekiel 1:26 KJV, which I shall prophetically interpret in the next section.

The Locus Trinitarian God

Now it is expedient to discuss and to verify that the Father, the Son, and the Holy Ghost coexist as one and that they occupy the same space, which manifests them as the Trinitarian God. One of several scriptures that support this biblical claim is in the book of Ezekiel.

> And above the firmament that *was* over their heads *was* the likeness of a throne, as the appearance of a sapphire stone: and upon the likeness of the throne *was* the likeness as the appearance of a man above upon it. And I saw as the colour of amber, as the appearance of fire round about within it, from the appearance of his loins even upward, and from the appearance of his loins even downward, I saw as it were the appearance of fire, and it had brightness round about. As the appearance of the bow that is in the cloud in the day of rain, so *was* the appearance of the brightness round about. This was the appearance of the likeness of the glory of the Lord. And when I *saw* it I fell upon my face, and I heard a voice of one that spake (Ezekiel 1:26–28 KJV, emphasis added).

My interpretation of Ezekiel 1:26–28 is that this biblical visual aid, a sapphire stone, *is God—a Spirit and the Word.* It includes the Word because "sapphire stone" is a gem variety that has colors. This is unlike God alone, a Spirit. We learn in the Bible that "the Father himself, which hath sent me, hath borne witness of me. Ye have neither heard his voice at any time, *nor seen his shape*" (John 5:37 KJV, emphasis added). Also, in Revelation 4:5 KJV, God's seating includes jasper and a sardine stone. Therefore, He alone, a Spirit, is not seen sitting. However, His spiritual appearance is biblically noted in the expression of moving and walking. We learn in the Bible that "[i]n the beginning God created the heaven and the earth. And the earth was without form, and void; and darkness *was* upon the face of the deep. *And the Spirit of God moved upon the face of the waters*" (Genesis 1:12 KJV, emphasis added). We also learn in the Bible that "they heard *the voice of the Lord God walking in the garden in the cool of the day*: and Adam and his wife hid themselves from the *presence of the Lord God* amongst the tree of the garden (Genesis 3:8 KJV, emphasis added). Most likely, they would have seen His shape, or another transcendent form of Him. In the next portion of my book, I shall also discuss God in the context of motion. However, for now, this adjacent physical-man-like appearance in Ezekiel 1:26–28 *is Jesus*. And the appearance of fire around and within this Trinity, in Ezekiel, is *the Holy Ghost. Actually, in retrospect, I can say they all three occupy the same space at the same time—the throne.* And for proof that they are one, according to Ezekiel, Ezekiel had concluded and written that these three when together in their separate spirit forms were the presences of the likeness of God's glory (One God) (Ezekiel 1:27–28 KJV). According to John, in the book of Revelation, these three were also present as one.

The three who are present are the Father, the Son, and the Holy Ghost. However, the only visible individual is Jesus Christ of Revelation, standing alone. In Ezekiel 1:26–28, they appear separately on the same throne. They arise as one from Ezekiel's expressed throne. They take the route to John's standing position in the book of Revelation. These same three, in Revelation, having been mobile, are now one body, Jesus. He is seen standing in the midst of the golden candlesticks. The living being in Revelation 1:13–16 is God, a spirit. The visible physical feature(s) in this detailed scripture are of Jesus, the Word, and the Son of man, who is also the Ancient of Days. And the brightness that is expressed within his eyes is the fire within him. It is the in-dwelling Holy Ghost. Interpreting, this is Jesus Christ of Revelation, the Trinitarian *God*. Remember, God is a Spirit. He is not in need of clothes. The Ancient of Days has physical features. Therefore, He would be the recipient of attire.

Jesus is the self-transforming Word. It is He. The youth stated this in my classroom that day—as John, Daniel, and Isaiah also have emphasized.

God, the Word, and the Holy Ghost are *one deity*. They also occupy the same space at the same time. We learn in the Bible that "There are three that bear record in heaven the Father, the Word, and the Holy Ghost: and *these three are one*" (1 John 5:7 KJV, emphasis added).

Jesus Is the Transcending Word …

Another biblical example of the Word's transcending power is when Moses asked the Lord to show him His glory. Acknowledge now that God is a Spirit and, therefore, does not have a face or hands or back parts. And therefore, no doubt, most likely, it was the Ancient of Days who said to Moses he could not bear to see him in His glorified form.

> And he said, Thou canst not see my face: for there shall no *man* see me and live. And the Lord said, Behold, *there is* a place by me, and thou shalt stand upon a rock: And it shall come to pass, while my glory passeth by, that I will put thee in a clift of the rock, and will cover thee with my hand while I pass by: And I will take away mine hand, and thou shalt see my back parts: but my face shall not be seen. (Exodus 33:20–23 KJV, emphasis added)

These details also give heed to the biblically interpreted statement that Jesus is the expressed image of the invisible God. We read in the Bible, "Who being the brightness of *his* glory, and the expressed image of his person" (Hebrews 1:3 KJV, emphasis added). The subject here is the seeing of the glory of God in the face of God. According to the previous scripture (Ezekiel 1:26–28 KJV), when sitting as three upon the throne, they are the likeness of God's glory. The full glory of God then consists of a sapphire stone, a man, amber, and fire. So biblically, interpretatively, the glorified physical state of God is the Ancient of Days, who is the Trinitarian God.

Note the one who continues to sit on the throne is the Ancient of Days. He is the Word, who resides in and stepped forth out of the bosom of God (John 1:18). Revelation 6:15–16 (KJV, emphasis added) is an excellent example of the Ancient of Days sitting on the throne:

> And the kings of the earth; and the great men, and the rich men, and the chief captains, and the mighty men, and every bondman, and every free man, hid themselves in the dens and in the rocks of the mountains; And said to the mountains and rocks, Fall on us, and hide us from the *face* of him that sitteth on the throne, and from the wrath of the Lamb.

The word *sitteth* in this scripture context refers to one who continues to sit. Isaiah uses the word *sit* in the same context as John in the book of Revelation uses the word *sitteth*. And this also means one who continues to sit. Isaiah recorded, "In the year that King *Uzziah* died I saw also the Lord sitting upon a throne, high and lifted up, and his train filled the temple" (Isaiah 6:1 KJV, emphasis added). In the physical interpretation of Isaiah's wording of seeing the Lord, it is implied that he also saw the Ancient of Days. Again, God is a Spirit who rests, resides, moves, or hovers over. Therefore, He does not have need of a train. It is the Ancient of Days who would be the recipient of a train. This is the garment that fills His temple. And the Ancient of Days is He who would also be seen sitting, as stated in Revelation 20:11.

Then, He who continues to sit also has red eyes, according to Revelation 1:14 KJV. In the following scripture, He is in several of His multiplex forms. There are numerous factors that support this. One is He wears many crowns on His head. The second is no one knows the complexities of His name. And the third is it is stated that He is the Word.

Revelation 19:11–16 KJV (emphasis added) reads,

> And I saw heaven opened, and behold a white horse; and he that sat upon him *was* called Faithful and True, and in righteousness he doth judge and make war. *His eyes were as a flame of fire*, and on *his head were many crowns*; and he had *a name written, that no* man knew, but he himself. And he *was* clothed with vesture dipped in blood: *and his name is called The Word of God* … and he treadeth the wine press of the fierceness and wrath of Almighty God. And he hath *on his vesture and on his thigh a name written, KING OF KINGS, AND LORD OF LORDS*.

In summary, the Word rides in all power. He rides in the raw, which is His visible and invisible transcending spiritual forms. These are not limited but are inclusive as follows:

- The Spirit of God (Genesis 1:2 KJV)

- The Word who resides in the bosom of God (John 1:8 KJV)
- The Holy Ghost (Hebrews 3:7 KJV)
- The Son of God (Revelation 2:18 KJV)
- The Ancient of Days (Daniel 7:9 KJV)
- The Spirit of Truth (1 John 5:6 KJV)
- Jehovah with its many names (Psalm 83:18 KJV)
- The seven spirits of God (Revelation 5:6 KJV)
- Melchisedec (Hebrews 7:3 KJV)
- The Man Christ Jesus (1 Timothy 2:5 KJV)
- Christ (Matthew 16:16 KJV)
- Jesus of Nazareth (Acts 10:38 KJV)
- The Lamb of God (John 1:29–36 KJV)
- The One who has trodden alone (Isaiah 63:3 KJV)
- A rod out of the stem of Jesse (Isaiah 11:1 KJV)
- The root and the offspring of David (Revelation 22:16 KJV)
- The Bright and Morning Star (Revelation 22:16 KJV)
- The Lion of the Tribe of Judah (Revelation 5:5 KJV)
- The Son of David (Matthew 10:46–47 KJV)
- One who looks like unto the Son of Man/God (Matthew 8:20 KJV and Daniel 3:25 KJV)
- The Word who rides the white horse (Revelation 19:11–16 KJV)

This list of scriptures certifies that God, the Word, has multiple identities. And in the mind of God, each transcending form has a specific duty with power. This is based on stated conditions before the foundation of the world. Remember, all things in heaven and in earth were created by Jesus and for Him (1 Colossians 1:16). The Bible confirms Jesus's absolute transcending divinity in the book of Hebrews. We read the following in the Bible: "and upholding all things by the word of his power, when he had by himself purged our sins, sat down on the right hand of the Majesty on high" (Hebrews 1:3 KJV). And this is why He properly exalts his Word higher than his name(s). Psalm 138:2 (KJV) says, "I will worship toward thy holy temple, and praise thy name for thy loving kindness and for thy truth: for thou hast magnified thy word above all thy name." This thesis has revealed God by way of a verbal dialogue, which actually occurred between teacher and students. And this narrative has revealed the particular character of his Spirit. These written scripts have also provided detailed discussions of certain particulars of His numerous names and how they relate to His transcending power and authority. Still, the innate knowledge that Jesus is God is given of Him. And more often than not, this knowledge comes with the support of other spiritual occurrences. The following are my personal experiences of how I came to comprehend and to know that Jesus is *the Trinitarian God and the Only Self-Made Man*. Come; follow my footsteps further into my written Spirit-filled adventures with the Logos.

My Godly Experiences
inside the Locus

These short narratives are my real-life adventures. When I was around age nine, a forgotten miracle happened to me. I was taught how to swim by a male stranger. It was a scorching summer's day in Winston-Salem, North Carolina. My two younger brothers and I had chosen the long walk to our favorite swimming pool. I remember this clearly. The sun was beating down heavily upon us like floods of rain that offered no shelter. Our feet suffered dearly. We repeatedly said, "Ouch!" as our feet hit the hot pavement. We arrived at the public pool and showered. We decided next to test our swimming ability in the kiddie pool. We soon tired and left that pool to head for the big people's pool, as we called it. I tried, tried, and tried to swim! I finally gave up. I got out of the water and rested on the right edge of the shallow part of the pool. From within, I sadly said, "I want to swim." Peering straight forward, I saw a tall man approaching me. He stopped right in front of me. I said, "Take me over in deep, on your back." He said nothing. He just turned and offered his back to the little African-American girl. I climbed up on his back as one would a familiar friend's. We slowly approached the dividing line. I became tense. I said to myself, "How are we going to cross the rope?" I did not have the skill of breathing underwater. We did cross the rope without going underwater. We were a few paces from the rope, in deep. I felt excited! We turned around to face the shallow end. I soon found myself suspended in water. I never remember being let down into the water. I was just there, alone. Suddenly, I began to swim. I somehow swam past the rope. I knew that I had reached the shallow end because my feet hit the pavement. I stood up and looked back. I said, "I do not know him." I don't even remember his physical features. I just remember he was a man. I told my account to a class of students at Wayne County Community College (WC3). One peer approached me after class. She said it had to be the Lord who leaped inside me! My spiritual mother's interpretation was that my spirit was acquainted with God. But my flesh was not knowledgeable of Him.

At age twelve, I used to kneel in prayer. I did this on the side of my bed. I had a repetitive prayer because I had an inquiry of God. I wanted to know if He would heed my expectations of Him. Daily, I would say this prayer: "Lord, I want to see You. I want to talk to You. Lord, are they impossible?" I would say, "Make these manifest! Nothing is impossible for You. You have all the power." I did hope these would occur. I expected to see Him. I also expected to talk to Him and be with God Himself.

It happened. It was in the late 1970s when my friend and I sat on a bench. We were in Edinburg, Indiana, waiting for the Job Corps bus to come and retrieve us. All of a sudden, an African-American man in a clergyman's robe approached us. He was good-looking. He had the smoothest dark skin. He was attempting to persuade us to attend his church down the road. We did not like his vibe. We drew backward, as he moved forward to persuade us. To summarize, we said, "No." Out of nowhere, an elderly Caucasian man appeared. He was walking from the bench across from us. He approached us. He said the man should not say anything to us. We did not believe in Martin Luther King Jr. and Malcolm X.

I boldly said, "We do believe in Martin Luther King Jr. and in Malcolm X!"

He said, as a lady, I was a devil. I was promiscuous at a very young age. But for many years, I had been running on cruise. I had no comment. He said I did something to him every time he looked into my eyes. He was gazing into my eyes as if to view my soul. He then said the most profound words that led me toward a Godly converted life. He asked me if I believed that the truth is the light and that the light is the way of life. I said, "Yes. I do believe that the truth is the light. And the light is the way of life!" He asked me next if it was important to tell the truth. And I said, "Yes. It is important that you tell the truth!" He asked then if I would be his daughter. I said to myself, "I don't know why you want me to be your daughter. I don't know you no way." He said something immediately after my thought. He said he did not have a daughter. His tone of asking sounded so wanting.

I repeated his words. I said, "You don't have a daughter?" I felt sad for him. I said, "Okay, I'll be your daughter." Our bus came immediately after that. We just took off. You may wonder what happened to the first man. Well, as soon as the other man engaged us in conversation, he ceased to say anything. He took off, somewhat gliding toward the church he attempted to persuade us to attend. I wanted to stop him but not because of his good looks. Why did he leave when the other man came? His inquiries held our attention. My friend and I called him an old drunk man. We never smelled his breath. Nor did he sway. Neither did he swagger or stagger. When I told my spiritual mother, Mother Estella Boyd, she said, "He has multiple daughters. He desired a particular daughter." We learn in the Bible to "Be not forgetful to entertain strangers: for thereby some have entertained angels unawares" (Hebrews 13:2 KJV).

You may say, "Why did he ask you to be his daughter? He has remarkable, supernatural daughters like Mary, Jesus's virgin mother. She had God's Son!" It says in the Bible, "And she brought forth her firstborn son, and wrapped him in swaddling clothes, and laid him in a manger; because there was no room for them in the inn" (Luke 2:7 KJV). She suffered the great humiliation of having a son out of wedlock. We read in the Bible, "Now the birth of Jesus Christ was on this wise: When as his mother Mary was espoused to Joseph, before they came together, she was found with child of the Holy Ghost" (Matthew 1:18 KJV). What about Mary Magdalene? She washed His feet with her tears. She dried them with her hair. "And he turned to the woman, and said unto Simon, Seest thou this woman: I entered into thine house, thou gavest me no water for my feet: but she hath washed my feet with tears, and wiped *them* with the hairs of her head" (Luke 7:44 KJV, emphasis added). Then there is Hannah. She received a son from God but not without great agony, bewilderment, and prayer. "Wherefore it came to pass, when the time was come about after Hannah had conceived, that she bare a son, and called his name Samuel, *saying,* because I have asked him of the Lord" (1 Samuel 1:20 KJV, emphasis added). And let's never forget Esther. She laid her life on the line for her people. She went before the king and was willing to parish. We read in the Bible,

> Then Esther bade *them* return Mordecai *this answer,* Go, gather together all the Jews that are present in Shushan, and fast ye for me, and neither eat nor drink three days, night or day: I also and my maidens will fast likewise; and so will I go in unto the king, which *is* not according to all that Esther had commanded. (Esther 4:15 KJV, emphasis added)

What about the prophetess Anna? She was a complacent prayer temple dweller. She expected to see our Lord and did.

> And she *was* a widow of about fourscore and four years, which departed not from the temple, but served *God* with fastings and prayers night and day. And she coming in that instant gave thanks likewise unto the Lord, and spake of him to all them that looked for redemption in Jerusalem. (Luke 2:37–38 KJV, emphasis added)

Sarah, the mother of faith, sacrificed her first most precious cherished gift of God, her husband. She gave Abraham as a husband to Hagar. Sarah received the promise of the Father, Isaac. She was a free woman. Conflict arose because of Isaac's inherited birthright in God. Sarah aggressively took the defensive position. She told Abraham to send Hagar and her son, Ishmael, away.

> And she said, Who would have said unto Abraham, that Sarah should have given children suck? For I have born *him* a son in his old age. And the child grew, and was weaned: and Abraham made a great feast the *same* day that Isaac was weaned. And Sarah saw the son of Hagar the Egyptian, which she had born unto Abraham, mocking. Wherefore she said unto Abraham, Cast out this bondwoman and her son: for the son of this bondwoman shall not be heir with my son, *even* with Isaac. (Genesis 21:7 KJV, emphasis added)

I have concluded God's preference of me in the book of Isaiah. God informs us, "For my thoughts *are* not your thoughts, neither *are* your ways my ways, saith the Lord. For *as* the heavens are higher than the earth, so are my ways higher than your ways, and my thoughts than your thoughts" (Isaiah 55:8–9 KJV, emphasis added). He will work, and who can still Him? (Job 9:12 KJV). "Behold, he taketh away, who can hinder him? who will say unto him

What doest thou?" My indoctrination into holiness was a phenomenon.

I was escorted and ushered into holiness by the Spirit of God. It was in 1978, early one summer Sunday morning, about a year after Job Corps. Two of my sisters and I had partied hard that night. We had gotten in late. To bed and sound sleep I went. I woke suddenly. It was like a Christmas tale. I woke not to the sound of bells, like in Charles Dickens's famous story *A Christmas Carol*. Nor did I awake to the sound of a rushing train designated to transport children to see Santa, as happened in the movie *The Polar Express* with Tom Hanks. But I woke early as if I had gone to bed viewing heaven. I said, "Where are my church clothes?" A particular skirt shot into my psyche, like a meteor falling from the heavens. I jumped up, excited, all bright-eyed and bushy-tailed! I rummaged through a particular set of attire. I found my mid-length yellow flowered skirt. I refreshed myself and took off toward East Side Gospel Tabernacle, Church of God in Christ. The pastor was Reverend Berry. It was strange how I had previously met Reverend Berry.

I first met Reverend Berry on a particular day. I was hanging out with an old female friend. Her sisters attended Reverend Berry's church. We had been or were leaving Duke's Play House, a bar. Nevertheless, we found ourselves standing right in the entrance of Eastside Gospel Tabernacle, Reverend Berry's church. My friend mentioned that he was approaching us.

I said, "Who?" I knew her sisters went to a church—but not the one we were standing in front of. After he reached us, we all spoke. He asked each of us when we were coming to his church. My friend said something like "Soon."

I said, "I'll come when I come."

He was pleased with my response. My friend's countenance changed from human to one of viewing a ghost walking down the street in broad daylight.

It was months later that I was awakened by God's Spirit that early Sunday morning. As stated, I awoke. I did refresh myself. Then I rushed down Lemay and up Kercheval Street to attend Reverend Berry's church. I reached my destination. I went to the side door of his church. I banged and banged. I had to get in. It was time. It was time for me to come in out of the rain. Marilyn Monroe did not know when to come out of heavy rain. This is according to my understanding of a phrase in Elton John's song about her as Norma Jean Baker. Elton John's song implied the heavy rains consumed her. I was coming out of my rain. I insistently stood at Reverend Berry's side church door, banging. I was discovered by Mr. Reed. He lived behind me. He had darted from the other entrance. He said that I was knocking on the wrong door. He was the uncle of my friend's sisters and hers by law. I don't believe that I am mistaken. I entered the church building. I was seated; I was soon taken aback in amazement. A young lady of my age flew from the choir stand. She seemed to be in an impeccable spirit. And this spirit seemed somehow to have attached itself to her. I said to myself, "I want that!"

I was like the gentlemen who had attended Reverend Jim Jones's church for the first time and said he was home. But for me, that meant holiness. I watched this young lady being swept off her feet. It was by the Holy Ghost. I was looking into the Spirit world. Their performance reminded me somewhat of ballroom dancing. This is when the male partner gently and gracefully whirls his female partner down the aisle. But her invisible dance partner's performance was much more intriguing, by far. I did not ask if that was God moving in her. Nor did I have to. Neither was I told. I just knew. I knew as Peter did when Jesus asked His disciples who He was. God Himself led me. I was overtaken that redemptive summer day in 1978.

I remember vividly tarrying for the Holy Ghost. I was frustrated. I did not get it immediately. I became even more agitated when Reverend Berry commented. He let the congregation know that I was desperate to receive the Holy Ghost. After that, I wanted to tell him off. I was at Reverend Berry's church about three months when a serious conflict arose. There I stood in an empty church. One other person appeared. I asked, "Where are the people?"

Then, this single person's voice spoke of what had happened. The second time I went there; the doors were padlocked. I did not know what to do. I had to receive the Holy Ghost. It is the best coming from God out of heaven.

> Another parable put he forth unto them, saying, The kingdom of heaven is like to a grain of mustard seed, which a man took, and sowed in his field: Which indeed is the least of all seeds: but when it is grown, it is the greatest among herbs, and becometh a tree, so that the birds of the air come and lodge in

the branches thereof. (Matthew 13:31–32 KJV, emphasis added)

"Again, the kingdom of heaven is like unto treasure hid in a field; the which when a man hath found, he hideth, and for joy thereof goeth and selleth all that he hath, and buyeth that field" (Matthew 13:44 KJV).

"Again, the kingdom of heaven is like unto a merchant man, seeking goodly pearls: Who, when he had found one pearl of great price, went and sold all that he had, and bought it" (Matthew 13:45–46 KJV).

So I was saddened by the absence of members and the padlocking of Reverend Berry's door. I learned much later his church did reopen. I had met my future spiritual brother. I met him when I had left the locked church doors. We were walking the same path. We were going in opposite directions. We connected on the slope of the sidewalk on Kercheval Street. It was a stone's throw away from the church. He began a conversation. He soon told me about Redeem Church of God In Christ. I was anxious to continue seeking God's truth, and it was a COGIC church. I went there and fell in love with their spiritual environment. Their burgundy curtains hung open and seemed to sway a little. Sister Faye sang "I Found Jesus" by Myrna Summers. I was so taken up in the Spirit of the choir's song I was literally so tempted to ask Sister Faye, "Where did you find Jesus?" I was flabbergasted and starstruck by the presence of God. No, I did not ask her where she found Jesus. So I did not miss a beat in my search for God's Holy Ghost and truth. One of my special friends was Rita T. My denomination was

COOGIC, and she was Apostolic. Back then, the mixing of these denominations was taboo. It was like trying to mix oil and water. We enjoyed walking down the street talking about God. It was she who reminded me that Jesus said, "Judge not." She reminded me, Jesus has commissioned us not to talk about our neighbors. This include whether our neighbors are good or bad. I am still working on that, Rita T. Although I had come in holiness in 1978, I did not receive the Holy Ghost until 1979. Rita T. assisted me on my course to receiving the Holy Ghost. She told me of a sanctified sister and a revival. We went. I got in line. The anointed female minister asked me what I wanted of God. I said, "The Holy Ghost." She asked me how you got it. I said, "By faith." I began to tarry. That meant shutting out all other activity, closing my eyes, and communicating with God. The female minister laid her hand on my throat, and she soon requested for me to let the Holy Ghost speak. I did not understand, but I was speaking in an unknown tongue and trying to control myself. After tarrying, I was asked if I got the Holy Ghost. I said that I did not get it. Back then, they did not tell you if you had received the Holy Ghost. You had to confess for yourself. My friend also asked if I had received God's gift. I told her no. The altar workers asked me, and I said that I would be back to receive the Holy Ghost the next day.

I went home, and while I was getting ready for bed, the Spirit said, "Nannette, you got the Holy Ghost."

I said, "I am going to get my Bible, and I am going to see if I got the Holy Ghost." I did not understand my reply. I just believed in that inquiry process. I reached for my Bible and somehow found the scripture I sought about the Holy Ghost. I read it. I began to say over and over, "I got the Holy Ghost." God's Word became His voice to me. I confessed to having the most precious gift of God. That gift is His Spirit living inside me.

My new pastor, Elder Willie B. Jackson, was friendly, and so were we. My pastor believed in fellowshipping with Apostolics when it was not popular. I remember clearly having a Caucasian band of individuals during one of our services. We thought it was cool and enjoyed the fellowship. I don't remember what their denomination was. We knew our pastor was a pretty good judge of character.

I am fast-forwarding my spiritual journey to 1992. I was attending the Church of Our Lord Jesus Christ (COOLJC). My newly converted sister and my mother were attending there. And almost every Sunday, the echo of pulpit pounding was clearly heard from a bishop, the presidia of the Church of Our Lord Jesus Christ (COOLJC). The church was Solomon's Temple. Bishop William Lee Bonner was the elderly energetic senior pastor there. He, with all his spiritual authority, would soulfully insist Jesus was God! After many encounters, I would often say, under my breath, "What else?" I meant I wanted him to preach something else about Jesus. And then, he would often divert and make known that Jesus was self-formed. He insisted that Jesus's self-creation was the root of Him. I finally began to grasp the concept that Jesus was God. This continual emotional pulpit message and pounding became a spiritual way of life. It became like breathing the freshest air. I was going somewhere spiritually; somewhere I had always wanted to go, further inside the Logos. As he continued to preach that Jesus was God, my thoughts of what happened to me at the pool began to surface.

I realized that COOLJC's doctrine was relevant to my swimming experience. It also supported what the young lady at WC3 said about the Lord jumping in my body. That happened during my swimming experience. Jesus had to transform from human to divine to get in my body. In an instant, He went from human flesh to Spirit. I realized He had converted from Jesus to God to reside within me. I resolved, that day, that He had to be God. Then the gratitude that comes with given knowledge and this swimming experience took precedence. A leap of faith in a transcending God became possible. Then, one day, a greater confirmation about Jesus's transcending powers came too for wishing. This occurred in discussions that Melchisedec was Jesus Christ. It took precedence. I continued to pick over the relevant scripture (Hebrews 7:3 KJV). The bulb that lights the mind where knowledge is discovered turned on. And somewhere within this time frame, all other expressed revealing concepts of Him began to fully surface inwardly by His Spirit. This occurred as a stretching out of my comfort zone maximized and stick-to-it-iveness stepped forth. When I began to accept whatever God revealed of Himself, these revelations came through His Word, His Spirit, and others. They became the basis for a closer walk in God. I no longer had to inquire, "Who is this old man in Revelation 1:14?" This experience and manner of teaching, preaching, studying, and discussing the Word became like breathing; it was on demand.

Confirming Remarks and Introduction to Sermon Nets

So far, in this portion of my book, I have interpreted and discussed the transforming of God the Word, who is God, a Spirit. I have strongly defended that the Ancient of Days is the Trinitarian God and therefore is the only self-made man, the man Christ Jesus.

Next are power-punching messages that edify Jesus the Word. After, I have incorporated a sprinkle of spiritual magic that seems to be heard in spirit-filled harmonic songs. I have engrafted particular song lyrics that reinforce that God the Word is who He chooses to be. And together, these assert the oneness of the Godhead bodily. Lastly, I shall continue to interpret and to validate why Jesus is the Trinitarian God and the Only Self-Made Man!

Sermon Nets of Jesus's Divinity

In this literary section of my book are sermon nets and a written documentation exalting Jesus God. I am going to paraphrase a powerful, stunning message I heard at a 1993 convention. The host church was the Church of Our Lord Jesus Christ (COOLJC). This breathtaking message about Jesus was articulated by an electrifying preacher. They told me the preacher was Pastor Jeremiah Jones. My version of his particular sovereignty of God follows. They are on the left side. My recall of his responses to God confessing His sovereignty is in quotes on the right. And the dialoguing is as follows:

> The Ancient of Days: "God said I know who I am!"

> Michael the Archangel: "How do you know God?"

> The Ancient of Days: "Because every time I say something it comes to pass!"

See! God said something to manifest Himself the Ancient of Days. Perhaps the Word, who is in the bosom of God, stated this command: *God the Word come forth!*

This next sermon net is literally a teaching clip that I discovered in *Tomorrow's World*, written by Roderick C. Meredith. Roderick C. Meredith's message of God's divinity is a masterpiece, an excellent conceptual view of the Logos. His written sermon net is a peripheral view of my written theory of Jesus. And his pertinent passage reads, "Most of these Pharisees were presumably sincere. They thought they were worshiping the God of the Old Testament—who actually was standing right in front of them as Jesus Christ, the 'Word,' now come in human flesh" (Tomorrow's World, 2014).

The next sermon net is a message by a famous Pastor. "The Great Revelation" was the core title of Pastor's sermon net. His message was taken out of Deuteronomy 6:4. The Pastor asserted that Moses said to Israel, "Hear, O Israel, the Lord our God is one Lord." His sermon of the absolute sovereignty of God was expressed in his sermon net.

The last selected sermon net is a direct Internet response. I have applied the total researched content because these scripture verses are identical to a few of mine. The Internet scriptures also confirm that Jesus is God. And this affirmation of Jesus's divinity was by an unknown correspondent. Their YouTube confirmation of Jesus's deity is as follows:

> Jesus Christ Is the Lord God Almighty and the Most High God!

Biblical Evidence That Declares that Jesus Is the Lord God Almighty and Most High God!

Proof Texts that Prove the Supreme Deity of Our God and Saviour Jesus Christ ... by Jesus Christ[1]

These Sermon nets were selected to confirm that Jesus is who He chooses to be from a sharing experience. Next are song lyrics, and they should be true writers of the lyrics. These song lyrics are labeled in memory of those selected ones who have departed, Soldiers for Christ (SFC). These songbirds who sing prove that Jesus, the Word, is who He chooses to be.

---

[1] Taken from the Internet, Author's Date, December 7, 2016, YouTube, Rev. 1:1, 1:17; Rev. 1:11a/Rev. 1:8, accessed July 2, 2017.

Encouraging Gospel Songs of Jesus's Divinity[2]

"Come Thy Almighty King" by Charles Wesley (1757)
"The Water Way" by Sister Hattie Edwards
"The Ancient of Days" by Jamie Harvill and Gary Sadler
"How Great Is Our God" by Chris Tomlin
"Days of Elijah" by Judy Jacobs
"My Everything (Praise Waiteth)" by
Richard Smallwood and Vision
"You Are God Alone" by Bishop Marvin Sapp
"We Praise Your Name" by Dr. F. James Clark
"I Am Going Away" by Bishop Walter
Hawkins and the Love Center Choir

"His Eye Is on the Sparrow" by Lyricist Civilla D.
Martin and Composer Charles H. Gabriel (1905)

---

[2] Song lyrics taken from *LetsSingIt* (the Internet lyrics database).

"Come Thou Almighty King"
Charles Wesley (1757)

Help us Thy Name to sing,
Help us to praise!
Father all glorious,
O'er all victorious,
Come and reign over us,
Ancient of Days!

In Memory of Bishop G. E. Patterson

"The Water Way"
Sister Hattie Edwards

There shall be light in the evening time
The path to glory you will surely find
Through the water it is the light today
Baptized in Jesus' name!
Young and old repent of all your sins
And the Holy Ghost will enter in
The evening time has come
It's a fact that God and Christ are one!

In Memory of Bishop W. L. Bonner

"The Ancient of Days"
Jamie Harvill and Gary Sadler

Blessing and honor,
glory and power
Be unto the Ancient of Days
All of creation bow before the Ancient of Days
You will be exalted, O God,
And your kingdom,
Shall not pass away.

In Memory of Mother C.

"How Great Is Our God"
Chris Tomlin

The splendor of a King
Clothed in majesty
Age to Age he stands
And time is in his hand
The Godhead, three in One
Father, Spirit, Son
The Lion and the Lamb

In Memory of Brother David B. Ford

"Days of Elijah"
Judy Jacobs

Behold he comes riding on the cloud
Shining like the sun
Prepare ye the way of the Lord
Lift your voice
Year of Jubilee
And out of Zion's Hills
Salvation comes
There's no God like Jehovah

In Memory of Elder W. B. Jackson

"My Every Thing: (Praise Waiteth)"
Richard Smallwood with Vision

Oh Lord, You're my everything
Praise waiteth for Thee my King
Oh Thou who hearest every prayer
You are my light
That shines in the midst of darkness
You are my help.

In Memory of Your Loved Ones

"You Are God Alone"
Bishop Marvin Sapp

There's no question of your greatness,
No searching of your power.
Now unto the King,
Eternal, immortal, invisible
Thee only wise God
Be all glory and honor,
Dominion and power forever

In Memory of Dr. Mattie Moss Clark

"We Praise Your Name"
Dr. F. James Clark

Honor and Power be
To the One above
Father, we worship you
Lord, You are great!
Lord, You are powerful!
Lord, You are mighty,
and we praise Your name!

In Memory of Mother Estella Boyd

"I Am Going Away"
Walter Hawkins

I'm going away,
To a place,
I'll live eternally,
Special place
Prepared just for me;
I'm going to see Jesus
In that bye and bye
And he's gonna wipe
The tears from my eyes

In Memory of Bishop Walter Hawkins, a Music Legend

"His Eye Is on the Sparrow"
Civilla D. Martin, Composer Charles H. Gabriel, and Bill Gaither (Lyrics)

"Let not your heart be troubled," His tender word I hear,
And resting on His goodness, I lose my doubts and fears;
Though by the path He leadeth, but one
strip I may see; His eye is on the
sparrow, and I know He watches me.

In Memory of the Great Evangelist
Billy Franklin Graham

Conclusion

In conclusion, I have debated and concluded that Jesus is the locus in His triune form. I have noted and listed particular reasons the Word of God transcends the self. God the Word transcended to manifest a visual picture of Himself, a Spirit. So, from God's bosom audaciously proceeded forward the Word of life, the Ancient of Days (John 1:18 KJV). This transcending allele is God's Begotten Son (Revelation 2:18 KJV), God, the Word, whose form and location are based on stated conditions. We must then interpret to comprehend another reason why God the Word quickened to a deity. It was to fulfill a desire to bring forth a prophecy. This prophecy to be manifest is found in Genesis. It asserts that God formed man with His own hands. We learn in the Bible that "there went a mist from the earth, and watered the whole face of the ground. *And the Lord God formed man of* the dust of the ground, and breathed into his nostrils the breath of life; and man became a living soul" (Genesis 2:6–7 KJV, emphasis added). The hands that formed the first man most likely were of the transcendent Word. It is reasonable then for God to manifest physical properties to form with His own hands that man of the dust. A third manifestation of the Word in transcending is depicted in God's creation of the *slain Lamb* of God.

This transcended Lamb stands before the throne of God to represent the transcended soon-coming redeemer. This description of the Lamb is in Revelation 5:6. And over two thousand years later, that Lamb came among us. We learn in the Bible that "The next day John seeth Jesus coming unto him, and saith, Behold the Lamb of God, which taketh away the sin of the world" (John 1:29 KJV).

Jesus is the interpreted purpose of the book of Revelation. That interpreted purpose is to reveal that He is God. We learn in the Bible that the book of Revelation is "the Revelation of Jesus Christ" (Revelation 1:1 KJV). And Revelation 19:11–13 asserts a summary of Jesus's Godhead authority. In this scripture, He rides the white horse in all He is, was, and is to come. This scripture also gives a pictorial description of Jesus's genetics transcending absolute dominance. Remember, we learn in the Bible that "there are three that bear record in heaven, the Father, the Word, and the Holy Ghost, and these three are one (1 John 5:7 KJV). And the three are the Trinitarian God. And since the Trinity is *only visually* expressed in Jesus, then Jesus is, for a fact, God (Revelation 1:7–18 KJV)! And He is the only self-made man (Colossians 2, 9 KJV).

The Word of God has pizzazz. The Word of God came in my room that summer's day in 1978. The Spirit of God woke me up, and it continues to carry me on a life-changing spiritual journey. I am being transformed by the potter into a vessel of honor for the master's use. When we walk in the Word of God, we are walking on God's spiritual highway. The Word of God is to be worshipped. It is to be honored whether it is in written form or Spirit form. The

Word is relevant whether it is expressed in the words of a child or adult. The Word is significant even if it is fine-tuned by a stranger sitting on the other side of your bench. It is to be practiced because we learn in the Bible that "It is written, Man shall not live by bread alone, but by every word that proceedeth out of the mouth of God" (Matthew 4:4 KJV). This dialoguing is an expression of His innate triune personality and spiritual/physical traits.

Now, here is some food for thought. In the book of Matthew, Jesus proclaims His spiritual position before completing His divine mission. We learn in the Bible that "Jesus said unto her [Mary], *I am the resurrection, and the life*" (John 11:25–26 KJV, emphasis added). Before the world, Jesus is the resurrection and the life. Then what position does God hold? We learn in the Bible that "Jesus came and spake unto them saying, *all power* is given unto me in heaven and in earth (Matthew 28:18 KJV, emphasis added). So, what power does God have?

We also learn in the Bible that Jesus asserts, "I am he that *liveth*, and was *dead*" (Revelation 1:18 KJV, emphasis added). So who is God? For a final dance, let us consider what Jesus said to Philip. We learn in the Bible that "Jesus saith unto him, have I been so long time with you, and yet hast thou not known me, Philip? He that hath seen me hath seen the Father; and how sayest thou then, shew us the Father" (John 14:9 KJV). Many have not seen him, but have been acquainted with Him through His Word. They have also experienced the Father. We learn in the Bible that "In the beginning was the Word, and the Word was with God and the Word was/is God" (John 1:1 KJV). The Word then becomes the Ancient of Days. He is also Jesus Christ of Revelation. He then transcends further, becoming the man Christ Jesus. Truly, God the Word is the place where life occurs. He is the set of all points that pertain to life and Godliness. He is the allele who transforms at any time and at exact expressed times. He is the Trinitarian God and the only self-made man—"Jesus Christ *the* same yesterday, and to day, and for ever" (Hebrews 13:8 KJV, emphasis added). Jesus Christ the same has endless possibilities. Jesus Christ the same has limited possibilities. Has Jesus's deity been proven? Like Andrea Crouch expressed in a written song, "Let (this) Church say, *Amen.*" For all others, "And it shall come to pass in that day, that the light shall not be clear, nor dark: But it shall be one day which shall be known to the Lord, not day, nor night: but it shall come to pass, that at evening time it shall be light" (Zechariah 14:6–7 KJV). "It shall be light in the evening time" (KJV).

Citations

Church of God In Christ: Statement of Faith, (www.gstcogic. org), accessed September 20, 2017.

Frank Charles Thompson, DD, PhD, Thompson Chain-Reference Bible KJV (Indianapolis, IN: B. B. Kirkbride Bible Co. Inc., 1988).

Jeremiah Jones, Pastor, Church of Our Lord Jesus Christ (Convention 1993).

"Jesus Christ Is the Lord God Almighty and the Most High God! Biblical Evidence That Declares that Jesus Is the Lord God, Almighty and Most High God! Proof Texts that Prove the Supreme Deity of Our God and Saviour Jesus Christ ... by Jesus Christ," Author's Date, December 7, 2016, YouTube, accessed July 2, 2017.

"Theology: The Doctrine of God," *The Nature of God*, Theology: 1, bible.org, https://bible.org/seroes[age/50. theology-doctrine-god, accessed June 22, 2018.

References

Ames, R. A. (2014, September/October). "Watch the Middle East" *Tomorrow's World*, 18-25.

Meredith, R. C. (2014, September/October). Which Jesus Do You worship? *Tomorrow's World*, 5-10.

Merriam-Webster's Eleventh Edition Collegiate Dictionary. Springfield, MA: Merriam-Webster, Incorporated, 2012.

The Thompson Chain-Reference Bible. Fifth Improved Edition. B. B. Kirkbride Bible Company, Inc., 1988.

About the Author

She was born in Winston Salem, North Carolina. She received her Master's Degree of Science in Human Services through Capella University. She is the daughter of Willie and Nancy Heath. She is the sister of 6 siblings. She has been spiritually taught by the best. Her first instructor is the Spirit of God. He ushered her to His House of prayer that summer's day. Her second spiritual family was The Church of God in Christ (COGIC). They taught her to be sound in faith, stay rooted and grounded in prayer and in the Word. Most of all is true to you.... Her third spiritual influence was her spiritual Mother, Mother Estella Boyd. She prophesied author's enclosed revelations. The particular two prophesies that are written in this manuscript. She told her their significance. Her fourth spiritual influence was The Church of Our Lord Jesus Christ (COOLJC). Their doctrine of Jesus gave her a preview that Jesus is God, although He is Son." A result, in COOLJC, she reached a spiritual maturity. A spiritual growth, she "had never known." This development was possible because she clings to those COGIC roots. She now experiences the sacred place Mother Boyd spoke of: "The divine place of no return." This is the spiritual traveling plateau that Isaiah

(35:8) speaks of. And this innate pavilion in God also gives her great sorrow. Nevertheless, with her anointing and with her "made up mind," every day she can give radical praise and say, "Alleluia."

Printed in the United States
By Bookmasters